IMAGES
of England

ASHTEAD

To Darling Li'l Sis & family —

— Never forget your roots.

All our love
Will, &m & family — XX

xxx.

Four soldiers from the University and Public Schools Battalion, Royal Fusiliers, at Sheaths Bakery, no. 49 The Street. They were billeted at Ashtead in 1914.

IMAGES
of England

ASHTEAD

Compiled by
Jane E.M. Jones and Ken Rogers MBE

TEMPUS

First published 1999
Copyright © Jane E.M. Jones and Ken Rogers MBE, 1999

Tempus Publishing Limited
The Mill, Brimscombe Port,
Stroud, Gloucestershire, GL5 2QG

ISBN 0 7524 1820 3

Typesetting and origination by
Tempus Publishing Limited
Printed in Great Britain by
Midway Clark Printing, Wiltshire

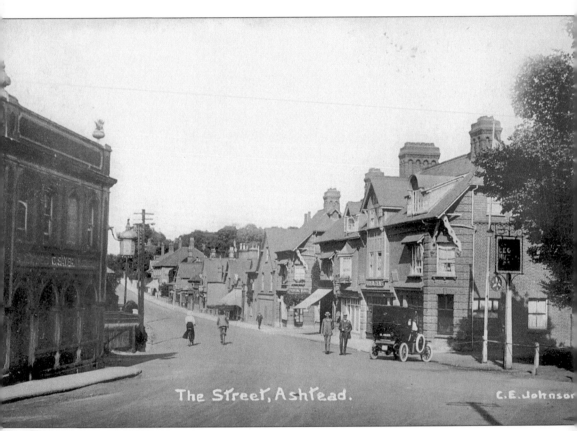

The Street, c. 1912.

Contents

The Forge, Rectory Lane, *c.* 1900.

Introduction

Ashtead today is a typical pleasant, small Surrey town in the so-called Stockbroker Belt, with a large percentage of its population therefore consisting of people who come to live in the town, and after a number of years move on. But it is far more than that.

It has a definite identity and a well recorded history of continuity and achievement going back hundreds of years. Those who move into the town quickly come to appreciate how much there is to this history and develop an affection for it, which compares well to the pride which is shown by members of local families whose history in the area goes back generations.

The recording of this passing history has been lovingly preserved by people born and raised in the town such as, for instance, Mr Meredith Worsfold, and we must be grateful for the stewardship of such families and individuals.

However, so many newly arrived families seem to develop quickly a similar fascination for the history of Ashtead. Why should this be? What is so special about Ashtead? The authors – father and daughter – who came to live here thirty years ago, hope this collection of old pictures, diverse facts and anecdotes goes some little way towards answering these questions. In short, however, it is simply that Ashtead is a really nice little town.

University and Public Schools Battalion, Royal Fusiliers, at the gates of Ashtead Park, Park Lane, in 1914.

One
The Street

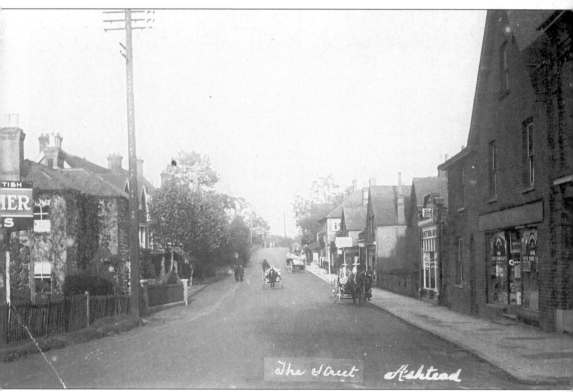

The Street, c. 1927.

Victoria Works, West Hill, *c.* 1926. Ashtead Potters Ltd started life at the Victoria Works in April 1923 under the driving force of Sir Lawrence Weaver and his wife Kathleen Purcell, Lady Weaver. They employed four disabled ex-servicemen. By 1926 production had increased and thirty to forty men were employed. From 1925 accommodation was provided for the potters in Purcell Close where a memorial to Lady Weaver stands today.

A selection of the pottery's wares was displayed at the Wembley Empire Exhibition in 1924, where King George V and his wife Queen Mary paid a visit. The Queen was a great collector of objets d'art (although rumour had it that she seldom paid for her acquisitions!) and she selected the dish on the left of the glass topped counter for her collection. Unfortunately the pottery did not survive the depression of the 1930s and it closed in 1935. Lime Tree Court homes for the elderly stand on the site of the pottery today.

Home of Joseph Payne, painter and decorator, *c.* 1912. This row of buildings was on the south side of The Street, later numbered 8-22. The couple on the right are probably Mr and Mrs Payne and the second woman is Mrs Florence Collings, aged about twenty-two. The sign over the door reads 'Painter and Decorator. Estimates free for general repairs.'

A bird's-eye view of The Street, *c.* 1900. This view shows the fields of The Leg of Mutton and Cauliflower farm on the right and The Street farm on the left. The house set back on the right was The Elms, a two-storey wooden building standing about 50 yards behind The Street, with access between nos 90 and 96. It was damaged during the Second World War, when a parachute bomb dropped nearby, and was rebuilt as a single-storey building.

NEW DAWN LAUNDRY LIMITED

ASHTEAD · SURREY
PHONE: 88

Laundering and Dry Cleaning

ALL WORK PROCESSED
by the most up-to-date plant, operated by an efficient staff.

YOUR SATISFACTION IS OUR OBJECTIVE

An advertisement for the New Dawn Laundry, 1950. This laundry was situated on the right of West Hill, a short distance past the Brewery Inn. The telephone number indicates how few telephones Ashtead had, even at this time.

The Brewery Inn, c. 1870. The inn started life as a small beerhouse in around 1800. The couple on the left are George Sayer and his wife Maria. George, a popular local man and a member of the Parish Council, was proprietor of the inn and the brewery situated behind it from around 1850 until his death in 1888. On the right, where the horse and wagon are standing, is the entrance to Woodfield Lane.

The Street and The Brewery Inn, c. 1890. George and Maria Sayer had many children, some dying in infancy and young adulthood. Their eldest surviving son, also called George, took over as manager of the brewery after his father. Around this time, as seen in this photograph, the building was extensively altered both inside and out, but there are still remnants of the original building at the rear.

The Leg of Mutton and Cauliflower, 1881. Dating back to the early 1700s, the inn, a combined farm and hostelry, has a history not only as a drinking establishment but also as a meeting house and a civic centre. Over the years it was used for meetings of the court baron and the coroner's court. The farm was credited with 73 acres, 6 acres lying to the rear of the inn but most of the land to the south of Barnett Wood Lane. Farm buildings stood near the inn and this photograph shows the demolition of one of these.

The Leg of Mutton and Cauliflower, 1903. The proprietor of the inn during the second half of the nineteenth century was Thomas Skilton, who lived here with his wife and twelve children. By the 1890s the present red-brick frontage had been added but even today there are still remains of the earlier timber framed building at the rear.

The Leg of Mutton and Cauliflower and Rectory Lane, *c.* 1904. To celebrate the relief of Mafeking in 1900, during the Boer War, a large bonfire was built in the centre of the village between The Leg of Mutton and Cauliflower and The Brewery Inn. The trees shown here caught fire and were badly damaged. The fine trees can be seen before the fire on p. 25. The damage was so severe the road was impassable and the mail coach from London to Portsmouth had to be diverted.

The Street and Rectory Lane, *c.* 1910. Elizabeth Farmer's Stores were to become the International Tea Company Stores soon after this photograph was taken, and were to continue trading for the next sixty years. The house obscured by the shop front was called The Cottage and was the home of John Hoyland, a beast salesman, who purchased the house in 1879 for £725. The shop front was added in the 1890s but the very pretty house still remains behind the present Alldays.

The Street, *c.* 1908. The hedge on the right of this photograph was the border to nos 40 and 38 The Street. The left-hand cottage of the semi-detached pair, no. 40, was demolished in 1930 to make way for the Woodcote Motor Garage, which was the first filling and service station in The Street. The right-hand cottage, no. 38, still stands today.

The Street and The Brewery Inn, *c.* 1953. The Brewery Inn had been rebuilt again, in the 1930s, when this photograph was taken, with the frontage which still survives today. The tree further down The Street on the left had stood since the turn of the century and was the last tree remaining by the shops. Sadly, that too succumbed to the increase in traffic and development and was destroyed in the 1960s.

The Street, *c.* 1905. The village policeman kept a close eye on the behaviour of local children and it was not unusual for a troublesome child to be arrested and appear before the magistrates, even for a crime such as carrying a catapult. Boys could also expect punishment from their teachers for misdemeanours occurring outside school. In 1900 two boys were caned by the head teacher of St Giles' School for stealing three oranges from the village grocer.

The Street from Woodfield Lane, 1925. This photograph gives a real impression of how open The Street must have looked before the building on the corner of Woodfield Lane appeared. At this time the shop second from the end, near The Leg of Mutton and Cauliflower, was a chemist run by Mr Gibbins. The premises are still used for a chemist's shop today, thereby continuing in the same trade for over three-quarters of a century.

The Street Farm, *c.* 1890. This farm stood on the corner of The Street and Woodfield Lane, with fields extending as far as Forest Lodge on the Epsom Road eastwards and northwards along Woodfield Lane to where the houses of Bramley Way and Meadow Road are situated today. The fields, with the exception of the one at the corner of Woodfield Lane, were sold off for building land in the 1890s and the farmhouse on the right of the photograph was eventually demolished to make way for the Esso service station.

The Street, *c.* 1920. The field on the left, in front of the house called The Shrubs, was used in the 1920s for grazing the dairy herd belonging to Sidney Wilcox. The dairy stood opposite, behind the open-topped bus, which the Wilcox family had taken over from Mr Kelsey. Mrs Wilcox worked in the shop and their two sons delivered the milk in a horse-drawn float, directly from the churn with a ladle. By the time of this photograph the trees outside The Leg of Mutton and Cauliflower had been cut down.

The Street, *c.* 1910. An extremely peaceful view of The Street clearly showing the field on the corner of Woodfield Lane which had belonged to The Street farm. The ivy-clad house beyond it, called The Shrubs, was home of George Sayer, son of George and Maria Sayer (see p. 13), who lived here with his wife Jemima and several children.

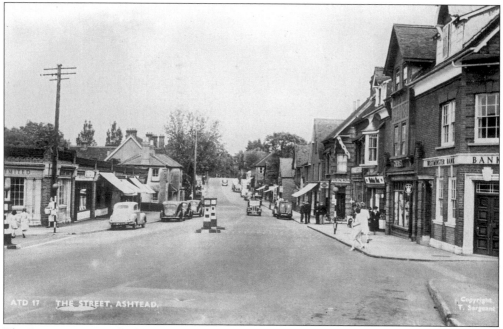

The Street, *c.* 1951. The last remnant of The Street Farm, the field in the previous photograph, had been built on in the 1920s. These shops stand where the dairy cattle once grazed. The Shrubs still remains, having been used by the Home Guard during the Second World War, but that too was soon to be demolished and replaced by two more shops.

On Thursday 24 September 1914, 2,000 men from the 21st Battalion, Royal Fusiliers (4th University and Public Schools Brigade) arrived in Ashtead. They made an impressive sight, with their public school scarves, college sweaters, golf caps (usually worn well over the left ear) and a badge on the lapel of their coats bearing the initials UPS.

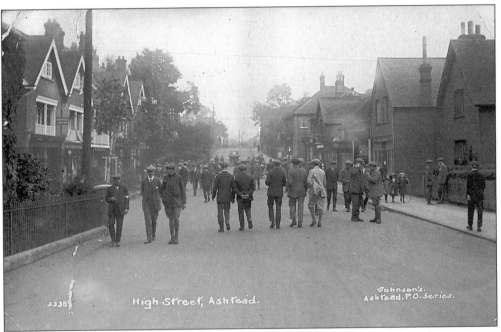

The men from the brigade were billeted in Ashtead for thirty weeks and their departure was met with genuine regret by local people. At 3s 4½d per man per day, the money spent on billeting alone for 2,000 men worked out at over £70,000. Large sums of money were also spent with the local tradesmen, providing a considerable source of income for the village. This postcard, sent by a recruit to his family, was among thousands produced locally at the time.

Post office staff, *c.* 1900. In 1895 Alfred Borer had become postmaster, running the post office from these premises at 78 The Street. In 1883, when parcel post was introduced, every letter carrier had to have their walk altered so the loads were not too heavy. Although the post office drew the line at carrying certain items, including 'gunpowder, live animals, and grossly offensive matter', this still left plenty of scope and the newly named postmen could find themselves carrying game, rabbits and fish along with their letters!

Post office staff, October 1911. Mary Stewart (standing in the centre) took over as Ashtead postmistress in 1908, running the post office from these premises at 51 The Street. Also in the photograph is Mr Berry, Epsom postmaster, with the beard, next to him is Mr Maynard and behind them are Charles Putland and Bill Stevens. The boys standing at the sides are Cates (left) and Frank Steere (right). In 1912 Harry Johnson took over the post office, moving it to his printing premises the following year at 58 The Street, on the corner of Grove Road.

The Street, *c.* 1900. The policeman is standing outside the post office at 78 The Street, run by Alfred Borer from 1895 until 1908. The sign above the door is also advertising the premises as a public telephone call office. In 1908 the post office moved to no. 51, which is the first shop on the right of the photograph.

HIGH STREET, ASHTEAD.

The Street, *c.* 1905. Many of the local businesses at the time made horse-drawn deliveries as shown here. The RSPCA kept a very close watch on the welfare of these working horses, often prosecuting neglectful owners. In 1899 William Gibbons appeared before Epsom magistrates charged with beating his horse at Ashtead. The defendant pleaded guilty but claimed provocation saying it had taken the horse five hours to travel five miles! He was fined £1.

The Street, 1950s. This is the same stretch of The Street as in the previous photograph, but fifty years later. The first building on the left, Gadsby's, remains relatively unchanged, but the pair of semi-detached cottages next to Gadsby's, whose gardens once edged the pavement, have had shop fronts added. The filling station on the right has also replaced The Street farmhouse.

The Almshouses, c. 1900. Situated at the east end of The Street, at the corner of Park Lane, these almshouses were built in 1738 from funds left by Lady Diana Howard, later Diana Fielding. They housed six widows in two rooms each and were administered by the Rector and trustees of Lady Diana's will. In 1852 Mary Howard provided funds to accommodate two more widows and also left £500 to be invested towards the widows' allowance after her death in 1877.

New Road, Ashtead.

Bench's Ashtead, Series.

The Marld, *c.* 1910. Called New Road at the time, it was developed with large villas in the 1890s. Until about 1830 an early eighteenth-century inn called the Berkshire Arms stood about where the Howard Memorial stands today. It was named after Sir Robert Howard's family; his father was the Earl of Berkshire. The village pound was also situated where Pound Court is today and the village stocks stood a short way into The Marld, on the west side, as late as the 1860s.

The Fountain, Ashtead.

R. Matten.

The Howard Memorial, *c.* 1915. The inscription reads 'This cross and fountain are erected in memory of the Honourable Mrs Mary Greville Howard by the parishioners of Ashtead and many other of her relatives and friends. She was beloved and honoured during a long life spent in doing good and mourned by all when taken to rest on 19 October 1877 at Ashtead Park aged 92. Her works do follow her.'

Two
South of The Street

Rectory Lane in 1900.

The Goblin Works from the air, c. 1970. Situated just off Ermyn Way and Green Lane near the Leatherhead border, Goblin (BVC) Ltd provided employment between 1938 and 1984 for many workers from central Surrey in the manufacture of vacuum cleaners and other household appliances. When it closed in 1984 the site was redeveloped as a large office block for the Esso Company. During excavations a Saxon burial ground was discovered.

Leatherhead Road, c. 1906. About 400 yards west of Ashtead village the turning on the right is Parker's Hill, leading to Ashtead Lodge. The signpost on the left indicates a footpath to Ottways Lane and a local polo ground which was kept mown by James Weller of Woodfield Farm. Colonel and Lady Howard are said to have ridden with the Hunt on the land south of Leatherhead Road, and after her husband's death, Mary Howard exchanged this land with an equal area in Lower Ashtead, owned by John Hackblock, a London merchant who wanted to entertain his friends with sporting activities.

Rectory Lane, *c.* 1914. Elizabeth Farmer had taken over Sharpe's grocery by the time this photograph was taken. Elevated advertisements were a feature of the time and those shown here were for Matten's Tea Gardens, situated in Rectory Lane, but easily accessible from The Street. Matten's was popular as a place of refreshment with the growing number of cyclists who would stream out of London towards the North Downs and beyond at summer weekends. Note the penny farthing bicycle on the roof of the shop.

Matten's Tea Gardens, Rectory Lane, *c.* 1910. This peaceful scene brings to mind a time of leisurely cycling on Sunday afternoons. It was not, however, always so peaceful. In June 1900 Henry White and Nellie Newdigg appeared before Epsom magistrates, charged with riding a tandem bike furiously down the hill by The Brewery Inn while Ashtead's residents were walking to church. They were told that if cyclists would indulge in the luxury of fast riding they must pay for it, and were fined 5s!

Fowler's Cottage, Rectory Lane, 1999. From the earliest times a route from Headley passed through the centre of Ashtead and then across Ashtead Common to Chessington and Kingston. Rectory Lane, known as Headley Road until the end of the nineteenth century, formed part of this route, so a number of old buildings are situated here. Built in the mid-seventeenth century, Fowler's Cottage is named after John Fowler, a builder and carpenter who lived here at the end of the nineteenth century (see p. 83).

Applebough Cottage, Rectory Lane, 1999. A neighbour of Fowler's Cottage, it could be even older, dating perhaps from the late sixteenth century. The building was once two cottages converted into one in 1954. At the rear is the old school house which was converted into Prosser's Laundry, being run by a brother and sister who lived in the cottage until the 1960s.

The Forge, Rectory Lane, c. 1909. From the 1870s George Wyatt owned the forge in Rectory Lane, the business being passed on to his sons James, John and George, who employed several wheelwrights, blacksmiths and apprentices. James and John Wyatt lived in the adjacent Forge and Wisteria Cottages until the 1930s. Members of the family can be seen standing in Rectory Lane in this photograph. The wall on the left is the boundary of the stables of The Old Rectory. The forge was in use until the 1950s and the houses of Blacksmiths Close stand on the site today.

Mr J. Wyatt, blacksmith.

Parkers Lane looking towards Rectory Lane, c. 1908. These cottages – now nos 1 and 3 Parkers Lane – formed part of the Howard estate. Originally one cottage, they are thought to have been built around a seventeenth-century structure. By 1838 Thomas Parker, who owned Ashtead Lodge on the opposite side of the road, and for whom Parkers Lane and Hill were named, had purchased the cottages.

The Crampshaw Works, seen here around 1900, was built in 1895 behind West Hill and adjoining Parkers Hill. Originally belonging to Mawson and Swan, by 1897 Cadett and Neal had taken over the building for the manufacture of photographic plate and paper. The Eastman Kodak Company took over the company in 1903 and five years later the plant moved away from the district. From the 1920s The Brifex Company produced leather cloth in the building, for bus and car seats amongst other goods. By 1972 the works had been converted into offices.

University and Public Schools Brigade, Royal Fusiliers, 1914. Taken at the corner of Grove Road and The Street, Harry Johnson, the photographer, entitled it 'A Merry Party'. Obviously taken at the same time as the photographs on p. 20, the men have borrowed a hoop from the little girl who was walking on the pavement on the right of The Street. Who the soldier at the front borrowed the baby from we shall never know!

Harry Johnson was village postmaster for about thirty-five years, running the counter from the family printing and stationery business at 58 The Street, situated at the corner of Grove Road. His father founded the business in 1894 and after his retirement in 1935, Harry was the sole owner until 1961 when he handed the business over to his son Norman. The arrival of the University and Public Schools Brigade in September 1914 led to a vast number of photographs of Ashtead being taken, and today we are greatly indebted to Harry Johnson for the record he made at the time in his superb quality photographs.

School Lane, seen here around 1900, was the name for the present Dene Road after the building of St Giles' School. The footpath on the left ran through fields until it met Grove Road, which at this time did not extend as far as Dene Road. If walkers did not wish to walk down Grove Road to The Street they could follow the path through the fields until it emerged in Park Lane, along the line of today's footpath.

Park Lane, c. 1938. Following the death of Pantia Ralli, Lord of the Manor, in 1924, and the subsequent sale of the Ashtead Park estate, property developers Maurice Chance and Frank Chown purchased the land to the west of Park Lane. The large houses in the photograph were built on this land in the 1930s. Oaken Coppice was also developed here, although not until the 1960s.

Park Lane, *c.* 1910. During the nineteenth century the only cottage on the West side of Park Lane was Park Cottage. For many years the cottage was used as a charity school but towards the end of the century Barrington Taylor, curate at St Giles' church, lodged here. He was curate for over forty years and died at Park Cottage in 1882, aged eighty.

Park Lane, *c.* 1910. One of these cottages pictured here was home in the late nineteenth century to James and Eliza Read and their four children. Eliza's son, Joseph Page, James' stepson, although partially paralysed since childhood, worked as a tailor, running his shop from the cottage. Before this, for many years, the family had lived in the old Ashtead workhouse, situated on the South side of Epsom Road at the Epsom boundary. Although it ceased to be used for its original purpose when Ashtead entered the Epsom Union in 1835, it was inhabited by poor families until its demolition in 1900.

Ashtead House, *c.* 1865. Standing in Farm Lane, this house was the residence of Captain Nathaniel Smith and his wife Hesther from the late eighteenth century. Their three surviving daughters remained unmarried; this was believed to be due to opposition from their mother, despite there being suitable suitors. George, their son, married a beautiful young woman, Sarah Hardman, who again was not accepted by Hesther. The marriage ended in disaster, Sarah leaving George with five young children, who were brought up by his mother and sisters at Ashtead House. The eldest son, also called Nathaniel, married and had two children. Elizabeth, their daughter, married Charles Denshire in 1841, sadly to be widowed twelve years later. In 1859 Elizabeth married the widower Revd William Denshire, her late husband's cousin, and with the marriage came eight step-children, six girls and two boys. The family are pictured below outside Ashtead House in 1861. From left to right: Elizabeth, Hester (aged nine), Isabella (thirteen), Mrs Smith (Elizabeth's mother), Emma (fifteen), Selina (eleven), Miss King (the governess), Mary (eight). Seated on the grass: Henrietta (aged six), Charles (four) and William (seven).

The wedding of Isabella Denshire and Henry Bailey, 8 November 1870. Isabella was the first of the Denshire daughters to marry. On the day of the wedding Mrs Denshire arranged for St Giles' School to be closed and the infant children to throw rose petals at the ceremony. On 24 July 1872 Selina Denshire married Charles Wilde, pictured below standing under what was reputed to be the largest tulip tree in England, which stands in the grounds of Ashtead House. Her brother William Denshire, aged eighteen, is standing on the left and four of her five sisters are attending as bridesmaids. The girls, from left to right, are Henrietta (aged seventeen), Mary (nineteen), Selina (seated, aged twenty-two), Emma (twenty-six) and Hester (twenty). The remaining Denshire daughters, except Emma, had all married by 1889. Emma Denshire, the eldest daughter, was considered to be the most beautiful of the sisters, but it is said she was jilted, and after this remained unmarried, inheriting Ashtead House on her stepmother's death, and living there until 1939 when she died in her ninety-second year. During the Second World War Ashtead House was used to quarter Canadian troops. Later it was subdivided, as happened quite frequently with large properties, to make more than one dwelling.

In the early hours of the morning of 16 October 1987, the most severe storm in living memory caused devastation in Southern England. Winds exceeding 100mph felled an estimated $1\frac{1}{4}$ million trees in Surrey, including this magnificent cedar tree, which stood in the grounds of Ashtead House. Although the storm was recognized as the worst since 1703, there have been other freak weather conditions recorded. In January 1877 Reverend William Adamson, rector of Ashtead, wrote to the *District Advertiser* telling them of an occurrence in the closing days of 1876. At about four o'clock in the afternoon thick snow began to fall immediately covering the ground and trees. Following a heavy fall all evening, by 2 a.m. 12-15in had fallen, accompanied by the sound of branches and even trees crashing to the ground beneath the weight. The following morning Revd Adamson walked through Ashtead Park with Mr Carlton, the head gardener, to see the destruction of many trees, including elms and oaks. Rev. Adamsom continued that none of Ashtead's oldest residents could remember such damage to trees caused by either snow or wind and he was interested to know how widely spread the snowfall had been. This last question reminds us how isolated residents were in the nineteenth century without radio or television to keep them informed of news outside their immediate area.

Three
Ashtead Park

West Lodge, Ashtead Park, *c.* 1910.

Ashtead Park House, *c.* 1900. In 1783 Frances Howard inherited the Ashtead estate and married Richard Bagot at Cavendish Square in the same year. Upon his marriage Richard Bagot changed his name to Howard. By now the mansion built by Sir Robert Howard in 1684 was in disrepair, and Richard and Frances Howard decided to rebuild it. The present house, shown in these photographs, was built on the same site to the design of an Italian architect called Bonomi. Richard and Frances Howard occupied the new house until their deaths in 1818, when their only surviving child Mary inherited the estate. In 1807 Mary married the Honourable Fulk Greville Upton who also assumed the name of Howard. He died in 1846 but his wife lived to the age of ninety-three. She was devoted to Ashtead, being especially generous to the poor who held her in the highest regard. As there were no children, following her death in 1877 the estate passed to a distant relative, Lieutenant-Colonel Ponsonby Bagot, who sold it after six years to Sir Thomas Lucas, a very wealthy industrialist, who lavished enormous sums of money on the estate.

A domestic servant in Ashtead Park c. 1890. Ashtead Park House was run by a small army of resident domestic servants. The census returns for 1851 show twenty-eight servants to look after the Hon. Mary Howard and her four visitors. These included a housekeeper, butler, cook, lady's maids, housemaids, footmen, coachmen, grooms, a scullery maid, a kitchen maid and washerwomen. The deer in the park once existed in such large numbers that culling was necessary every autumn and a deer slaughterhouse stood next to the stables. Deer can still be seen in the park today.

The West Gate Corner, Park Lane, c. 1930. When Sir Robert Howard built his mansion in 1684 he enclosed the park with a high wall. Large sections of the wall exist today, albeit at a reduced height. Although Sir Robert is recorded as not being particularly amiable, he was a gentleman of fashion and entertained royalty, including Charles II, James II and William III, in whose honour he named the gate which opens into The Park at the corner of Park Lane and Farm Lane 'King William's Gate', so the King could have easy access to Epsom race-course.

Park gates from Dene Road, *c.* 1905. When Sir Thomas Lucas purchased the estate in 1879, he had the north gate on the main Epsom Road altered, building commanding gates and a new lodge which was a replica of the West Lodge. Before this, North Lodge was similar to the smaller East Lodge.

East Lodge, *c.* 1914. Situated by the east gate of the park, this lodge was inhabited by estate workers. For many years in the nineteenth century, John Page lived here with his wife Mary and six children. John, an agricultural labourer, also held the position of parish clerk and was responsible for compiling Ashtead census returns. The Page family had lived in Ashtead since the early seventeenth century and John was a descendant of Samuel Page of Park Farm, referred to in Samuel Pepys' diaries after he stayed with him in 1663.

West Lodge, *c.* 1880. The gates of The Park were kept shut to prevent deer from straying and Sir Thomas Lucas offered the use of West Lodge to the headmaster of St Giles' School and his wife at a sum of £40 per annum, on condition that a boy or girl should always be in attendance to open and shut the gates.

The lake in the Park, *c.* 1917. When Sir Robert Howard built his new mansion house, he found that the estate had one great fault: the only water supply was from a very deep well from which water had to be drawn up by ponies. Sir Robert had the southern lake constructed to remedy the problem. It also must have been well stocked with fish as Sir Robert's account book for 1697 shows an entry for payment of 7s 6d to men for fishing the pond.

The bridge in the Park, *c.* 1937. This bridge at the foot of Rookery Hill, to carry the roadway over a dip, was one of the improvements Sir Thomas Lucas brought about during his time as Lord of the Manor. He also built two fine gravel terraces on the north and east sides of the house. Surrounding these, stone balustrades were erected, dividing the house from the grounds and preventing the deer from wandering right up to the house.

Alexandra Ralli was married to Peter Ralli of the famous Greek merchant banking family. She was widowed at the young age of twenty-seven and left with six young children when Peter died in 1868 at the age of only thirty. Alexandra bought Ashtead Park estate for her second son Pandias on his wedding to Argyro Sechiari on 3 August 1889. Pantia as he was known to his friends in Ashtead, a merchant banker like his late father, was only twenty-seven years old when he became Lord of the Manor. He was to become as popular as his predecessor Mary Howard.

Ashtead Park Estate, *c*. 1920. Mr Ralli was very sociable and was constantly holding parties with distinguished visitors such as Lord Kitchener. He had electricity installed throughout the house and lights were always lit along the drive when the Rallis went out at night. As well as a lift being installed in the house, a steam engine was put into the laundry which prior to this had always been worked by hand.

The boat-house from the lake, c. 1905. The northern lake and this ornamental wooden boat-house (also pictured below) were constructed for Pantia Ralli. One of the estate gardeners was paid a shilling a day extra in the winter to remove ice from the pond to the ice house. Pantia Ralli was a keen gardener, and his great hobby was growing orchids. He had many new flowers and shrubs planted and there was a species of almost every type of tree grown north of the equator in the Park. Shoots took place in the winter season and anyone connected with the village in an official capacity received a brace of pheasants and a couple of rabbits as a gift and when the annual deer culling took place in the Park, 8-10lb of venison was given as a Christmas gift from the Rallis. Mr and Mrs Ralli were both generous supporters of local charitable causes and Pantia once served on the Surrey Education Committee. They were often visitors at St Giles' School and gave the schoolchildren an annual Christmas treat of a party and entertainment, each child being given a bag of sweets and a new sixpence to take home.

The Head Gardener's house, now the headmaster's house, in Ashtead Park, c. 1906. The sundial over the front door dates this house to 1734. The Howards lived here in the 1790s while their new mansion house was being built. After this, the house became home to Ashtead Park's head gardeners. Against the north wall of its garden there were greenhouses 35ft long by 13ft 6in wide, heated by hot water pipes. John Hislop was Head Gardener in the Howards' time and George Hunt while Pantia Ralli was Lord of the Manor.

The cottage in the Park from a drawing by Ada Long, c. 1890. This cottage was the home of the estate bailiff and contained four bedrooms, a sitting room, kitchen, pantry and wash-house. There was also an enclosed yard with poultry houses. Although motor cars were in their infancy Mr Ralli was a great enthusiast and even had a cottage built on the estate for his chauffeur and garages for his eight cars.

West Lodge, *c.* 1906. The Chitty family, pictured here, lived in the West Lodge from around the turn of the century until the estate was sold in 1924. Edward Chitty worked as a gardener but in the 1924 catalogue of the sale of the Park, his son Arthur Chitty was described as living in the watchman's cottage. In 1907 Ashtead Park House suffered a burglary, the thieves entering by the butler's pantry window. They were however disturbed by a dog, escaping with only £150-worth of

articles. After this Mr Ralli organized a system of watchmen around the estate, who had an early key and clock system of recording where they had been. Despite this and the installation of electric alarms to the house several more burglaries took place. In one of these Arthur Chitty was quite seriously injured.

Kate Chitty of Ashtead Park, *c.* 1900. Kate, wife of Arthur who lived in West Lodge, worked as a housemaid in Ashtead Park House. Over ninety men and women were employed by the Rallis on their estate. Liveried footmen always stood in the porch to receive visitors, and servants in uniform accompanied Mr Ralli whenever he went out. However Mr Ralli had a reputation for showing every employee individual kindness and each year all his staff were treated to a feast in a marquee set up in the Park.

Ashtead Park House, 1920. Shown here is the committee formed to organize the construction of the Peace Memorial Hall. Seated in the front row are, from left to right: Miss Emma Denshire, Revd R.A. Waddilove (Rector), Mr and Mrs Pantia Ralli and Mr Marshall. By the time this photograph was taken Mr Ralli's health had begun to fail and on 5 February 1924 he died at only fifty-one years old. All Ashtead mourned, and the shops and schools closed as a sign of respect on the day of his funeral which took place at Norwood Cemetery. The principal servants, Mr Hunt (head gardener), Mr Morris (chauffeur), Mr Murrell (butler), Mrs Murrell (housekeeper), Mr King (steward), Miss Macbeth (head housemaid) and Mr Glazebrook (head gamekeeper) accompanied the family members with the funeral cortège as it passed through Ashtead Park. The route was lined with servants and their families and children from St Giles' School, who stood in torrents of rain. A memorial service was held in St Giles' church with an enormous attendance. As Pantia and Arghiro Ralli had no children, Arghiro sold the estate to the City of London Corporation to be the new premises of the Freeman's School and moved to live in a flat in Sloane Street.

Below opposite: Ashtead Park garden staff, c. 1900. Tending the extensive gardens of the Mansion House in Ashtead Park was an enormous task. Featured in this photograph are three members of the Chitty family, including Harriet the tea lady. A former gardener recalled looking for work after the First World War and initially being told by the Rallis there were no vacancies. However, The Rallis felt sorry for him as there was so much competition for jobs between ex-servicemen, and he was told that although they already had twenty-one gardeners, one more would not make much difference and he could be gardener number twenty-two!

Rookery Hill, *c.* 1957. The land between Rookery Hill and Epsom Road was purchased by Maurice Chance and Frank Chown in the 1924 sale of Ashtead Park. The area was only partly developed with large houses when a builder called Robinson purchased the remaining land and put forward plans to build 114 houses in the 1940s. Luckily it was recommended that no further development should take place here and in 1957 the land was purchased by Surrey County Council for the benefit of the public.

Filming of the *Benny Hill Show* in Ashtead Park. In 1985 technology beyond the imaginings of previous residents and workers in the history of the Park intruded into the normal summer routine. Film crews filming the Thames Television *Benny Hill Show* spent many days on location there. A long step from the horse-operated well of earlier years!

Four

The Lanes

Skinner's Lane, Ashtead.

Johnson & Sons
Photo Series. 21

Skinners Lane, 1913.

Ashtead Peace Memorial Hall, 1930. As was the case in almost every town and village in the country, a war memorial was erected in Ashtead sometime after the end of the First World War, but it was felt that there should be a memorial also to mark the peace. Ashtead Peace Memorial Hall was built on a plot of land in Woodfield Lane given by Mr Aubrey Marshall. The cost was met by public subscription, the Lord of the Manor, Pantia Ralli, leading the way with a gift of £1,000. The building was opened in 1924 and has been recognized ever since as a great social asset for the village.

Woodfield Lane, or Station Road as it was known at this time (1909), formed part of an eleventh-century way from Ashtead Woods to Headley. By 1638 it was a track which lay slightly to the west of the present road, the service road which is pictured here, and was known as Common Lane. Around the time of the coming of the railway the present road was constructed and it became known as Station Road.

Woodfield Lane, c. 1906. The oldest cottages in Woodfield Lane, probably seventeenth-century in origin, are now nos 33 and 35. Following the construction of the railway, in the 1850s, the road became popular with professional people commuting to London because of its close proximity to the station. So in the 1880s and '90s large houses began to be built. In the early part of the twentieth century the road became known as Woodfield Lane.

Woodfield Lane, c. 1917. Ashtead Cricket Club, on the right of this photograph, was founded in March 1887 and has seen many of Ashtead's celebrations over the years. In June 1911 it was the venue for the coronation celebrations of George V. After a special service at St Giles' church the Union Jack was raised on the green and the national anthem sung. This was followed by sports competitions and dancing in the evening. At 9.45 p.m. Ashtead's residents walked to the common to watch fireworks and the lighting of the bonfire at 10 p.m.

53

Ashtead fire brigade, 1920. This photograph of what looks like a hose cart must have been taken shortly before the abandonment of horse-drawn vehicles as motorized appliances were being introduced. The Ashtead brigade had a short life: it was founded in 1901 and merged with Leatherhead in 1926. The building featured is Gayton House, Greville Park, the home of the photographer John Payne Jennings, who could quite well have taken this shot. The fire station at the time was at Peto and Radford's Greville Works nearby.

Fred Bailey, an Ashtead fireman, 1920. Ashtead fire brigade, which would not have had a large number of calls, would probably have hired local horses for use as fire horses. It was recorded in some towns that when the fire bell rang, the fire horses would set off to the fire station themselves! The cost of hiring the horses at this time was about £1 per day and this would be added to the bill which the fire service would present to the insurers of any property which caught fire. Among other charges would be £3 for the first hour of the pump, £2 for subsequent hours and 3s for each fireman with an extra 2s-3s for each man as a turn-out fee, as long as they reached the blazing building within fifteen minutes.

Ottways Lane, c. 1905. Members of the Ottway family can be traced in Ashtead back to medieval times. John Lawrence's map of 1638 shows that William and Edward Ottway were tenants around the present Ottways Lane. In 1879 Frederick Peake, who had lived in Parsons Mead as a tenant since 1876, bought the property from Colonel Alexander Gleig. Part of Parsons Mead land was a field of glebeland between Skinners Lane and the present Maple Road. In the 1880s Frederick Peake gave the land for the building of four cottages for retired domestic servants.

The Paddocks, seen here around 1908, was a large house standing in five acres of land at the northern end of the older part of Paddocks Way. It was built for George Masterson, a race horse trainer and his horses. Also in the grounds were two cottages for racehorse trainers which still stand and are now called Hermon and Paddocks Barn. In the early 1960s The Paddocks was demolished and twenty-two small detached houses were built, forming Paddocks Way.

Skinners Lane, *c.* 1935. This thoroughfare appeared on John Lawrence's map of 1638 running into a track along the line of the present-day Ottways Lane. Skinners Lane formed the eastern boundary of the ancient Little Manor of Ashtead or Priors Farm, owned by Merton Priory. Consisting of 200 acres of farmland it extended to Harriotts Lane (then Barnards Lane), to the West, Barnett Wood Lane (then Marsh Lane) to the North and Ottways Lane formed its southern border.

Skinners Lane, *c.* 1910. In the 1880s George Masterson, the racehorse trainer who lived in The Paddocks, owned most of the land between Skinners Lane and Agates Lane. After his death in 1898 the land was sold off, leading to the beginning of the development in this area. Cottages such as Pleasant Terrace started to appear and at the same time medium-sized villas were built on either side of the lane.

Skinners Lane, *c.* 1909. This cottage at the corner of Gladstone Road still stands today although as the trees have grown it cannot be seen from the point where the photograph was taken.

H. Astridge Boot Repairs, Gladstone Road, here in the early twentieth century, was one of the many businesses in Ashtead run by the Astridge family. Gladstone Road, developed in 1902, was named by the builder, a Mr Taylor, who was a member of the council and a staunch Liberal. In the 1920s he also built Taylor Road which was named after him.

Pepys Cottage, Agates Lane, c. 1950. This is one of a number of Ashtead cottages to have been renovated since this photograph was taken. It is believed to be among the oldest houses in Ashtead, being late sixteenth-century in origin. It has now been developed into two dwellings. Although Samuel Pepys did visit Ashtead, it is thought neither he nor his family had any connection with the cottage.

Ottways Lane, looking east, c. 1910. The footpath signposted as leading to Ashtead station met Maple Road, the houses of which can be seen in the centre of the photograph, and continued into Skinners Lane. Ottways Lane was later widened and developed for residential housing and a telephone call box was erected near the position of the swing gate. Reg Dalton, a private in the UPS Brigade which was billeted in Ashtead during the First World War, wrote to his parents telling them he would sit at the end of this avenue of poplars watching the beautiful sunsets.

Footpath to Station Road, c. 1910. The footpath from Ottways Lane continued on through fields forming a network of footpaths through Ashtead's farmland, many of which have survived behind houses and gardens. This path either followed the route along what was to become Oakfield Road and then on to the station or branched eastwards through fields that were to become the recreation ground and onto Station Road, now Woodfield Lane. The stile still survives, albeit a little battered about!

The Old Cottage, Ottways Lane, c. 1953. This cottage standing on the south side of Ottways Lane is thought to date from the late seventeenth century. Around 1860 or 1870 it became known as Ordnance Cottage as it was rented by surveyors who compiled the first Ordnance Survey map of Ashtead in 1868. For many years around the end of the nineteenth century and beginning of the twentieth, it was used as a bakery with deliveries made to houses by a donkey and cart.

The Hut, c. 1910. This was situated at the end of a private avenue of poplars, on the south side of Ottways Lane, opposite Agates Lane. It was built in 1876 and the first resident was Colonel Alexander Gleig of the Royal Artillery, a veteran of the Crimean War, formerly in residence at Parsons Mead. He lived here with his wife Jessie, a cook, parlourmaid and housemaid. By the 1880s Colonel Gleig was living in Murrays Court, the former New Purchase farmhouse in Agates Lane, and The Hut had a string of notable owners including William Maples, chairman of the Parish Council. Although The Hut has been demolished one poplar tree remains from this beautiful avenue.

Ottways Lane, Ashtead.

Bench's Photo Series.

Ottways Lane in around 1910, showing the buildings of West Farm in the background. West Farm lay west of the Harriotts Lane and Ottways Lane junction. Credited in 1861 with 400 acres of arable and pastureland, James Harriott lived in the farmhouse with his wife, son and daughter employing twelve men and four boys. After James Harriott's death in the 1860s, his son Peter took over the farm, living in the farmhouse with his wife Eliza. In 1879 the house comprised four bedrooms, drawing, dining and breakfast rooms, flower gardens at the front and kitchen gardens at the rear. Eliza tragically died young, leaving Peter a widower with seven young children. By 1891 Peter had remarried, his new wife, Mary, having one daughter Dorothy. Although all the farm buildings in this photograph have been demolished and the area developed, the farmhouse still stands at 75 Harriotts Lane.

Harriotts Lane, c. 1932. In the 1920s West Farm was sold off for building. George Baker sold house plots along Harriotts Lane, building for himself a large house on the site of West Farm yard, called The Pantiles. This still stands today as a residential home for the elderly. He also developed the east side of a road through the farmland, calling it West Farm Avenue.

Five
Lower Ashtead

Barnett Wood Lane, c. 1910.

Woodfield Farmhouse, c. 1903. Formerly named Craddock's Farm, after the farmer John Craddock, Woodfield Farm was the last working farm in Ashtead by the late 1920s. This farmhouse stood on the site of the garage at the corner of Craddocks Avenue and Woodfield Lane. Its 150 acres of land were divided by the railway in 1858, connected by a footpath, now between Overdale and St Stephen's Avenue, known as the cattle creep.

Woodfield Lane, c. 1913. Beyond the coal storage shed is the turning into a footpath which ran across fields and led to the Epsom Road near Forest Lodge. This was later to become Meadow Road and Bramley Way. The handcart belonged to T. Steer, a shopkeeper of Barnett Wood Lane (see page 75), and was specially borrowed for the photograph. The man pushing it was one of Ashtead's characters, a Jack-of-all-trades, who went to the local 'tin chapel' on Sundays and hummed the hymns instead of singing them. The children rather irreverently called him 'humming Jesus'.

Old Barns, Woodfield Farm, *c*. 1930 (from a painting by Miss Catchpole of Ashtead). These timber-framed farm buildings stood in Woodfield Lane until June 1977. The stables still had the name 'Sweet Sue' legible on a stall door. After their demolition the land was used for residential development.

Craddocks Lane from Woodfield Lane, *c*. 1926. The course of Craddocks Lane followed that of the later Craddocks Avenue for some distance but veered slightly to the left instead of the right and provided pedestrians with access to the foot crossing over the railway and then onto the Wells Estate. The shadowy building on the near right was the granary of Woodfield Farm. It contained wooden bins for the grain and children often climbed up the ladder to the loft to play there. The building in the centre was a cow shed and behind that was the entrance to the farmyard. The notice in front of the oak tree reads 'Ashtead Football Club'. The pitch was in the field on the left, known either as Home Meadow or Station Meadow, and cows grazed there when there was no football.

Craddocks Parade, *c.* 1952. This area was developed in the 1930s on the land of Woodfield Farm, formerly Craddocks Farm. John Craddock and his wife Jane tragically lost their daughters in infancy and their son John died at the young age of twenty-three in 1814. With no son to carry on the farm, on John's death in 1821 the farm passed out of the occupancy of the Craddock family and by 1841 James Ballinghall was farming what was now Woodfield Farm.

Overdale, *c.* 1936. In 1935 the roads of Overdale, Culverhay and Broadhurst started to be built on the fields of Woodfield Farm north of the railway. The commuters, for whom the houses were intended, found they could buy properties cheaper and nearer to London, in places like Worcester Park. Even though the builders started to build slightly cheaper semis, many of the plots were not built on by the outbreak of the Second World War. To assist the war effort pigs were kept on the vacant sites.

The Fishpond, Ashstead Common.

The Pond, c. 1919. Old maps show a pond at the corner of Woodfield Lane and Barnett Wood Lane which has been in existence for hundreds of years. In the seventeenth century it was known as Oxmoor Pond, probably after the oxen which grazed on the nearby Woodfield. In the nineteenth century the hamlet of Woodfield ran from opposite St George's church to the Rye Brook, in front of which the soldiers of the University and Public Schools Brigade were parading, below, in 1914. Inhabited by agricultural workers, life was very hard for the poor families who lived in these cottages. Having many children and often lodgers, the overcrowded conditions led to sickness and a high mortality rate. In the background of both photographs can be seen the buildings of Woodfield Farm. The beautiful avenue of horse chestnut trees, on the far side of Woodfield, so much a part of the area around the station, were planted by Pantia Ralli, to make a pleasant impression when his guests arrived by train.

The Pond in 1908, looking southwards towards the cottages built by Job Curwood, a well-known Ashtead builder, in 1894. Local children were fond of wading out into the pond, but there has always been a problem with broken bottles and other dangerous objects being thrown in. Around the end of the nineteenth century, children skated on the pond during cold winters at a time when it was twice as big as it is today and was used for watering horses.

The Pond, c. 1960. The buildings of Woodfield Farm have now been replaced by the shops of Craddocks Parade, built in 1938 on the site of Woodfield Farm yard. A petrol and service station stand where the farmhouse once stood. The pond still remains a picturesque feature; until about 1990, a pair of swans would regularly nest there and successfully bring up a brood of cygnets.

Woodfield House Corner, Ashtead Common, *c.* 1909. This was the site of many a school outing in the summer months, especially on bank holidays, where the large building on the left, Woodfield House, was used as a refreshment centre. Adjacent to Woodfield House was a children's playground with swings, a helter-skelter, coconut shies, a roundabout, a sweet stall and a toy shop. The owners claimed to be able to seat 2,500 people in the refreshment rooms and marquees. Children played on that part of the common known as Woodfield and went rambling with their parents or teachers on the higher part of the common, known locally as 'the woods'. The clumps of elm trees shown in the photograph were felled about twenty years later, after a child was injured by a branch. Woodfield House, shown clearly below in 1909, also served as a bakery for many of Ashtead's residents. The baker at this time was Frederick Felton but the business was later taken over by W.H. Chaney, who displayed a large banner: 'The Children's Caterer' across the front of the house.

Schoolchildren, such as these boys from Peckham Rye pictured in 1902, often visited Ashtead Woods on day excursions. Arriving by train at 10.30 a.m., the party of 100 boys left their coats and satchels at The Rosery Tea Rooms on the common and spent an hour and a half playing rounders or cricket in the field behind the house. At midday, lunch was eaten in the open sheds and in the afternoon each class left with their teacher for a long ramble through the woods.

The boys, used to town life in Peckham, wrote later how they had enjoyed nature studies, watching wild rabbits, snakes, butterflies and even found goats, pictured here. After an enjoyable sham fight against the Boers, the party arrived back at The Rosery in time for a plentiful tea made by Mrs Curnow. After tea the boys spent a quiet hour or two collecting frogs and newts from the stagnant pools near the railway station, before the journey home to Peckham by train.

Ashtead Woods, c. 1907. There was a constant problem of poaching in Ashtead Woods. This became so prevalent that during the winter of 1900/01 there were so many arrests for rabbit poaching that the local paper reported an incident in February 1901 under the heading 'Those Rabbits Again'. Percy Glazebrook, head gamekeeper for Pantia Ralli, saw George Mills and Thomas Smith with nets over rabbit burrows on land over which Mr Ralli had the right of shooting. Whilst the two men were being detained an under-gamekeeper was assaulted. On appearing at Epsom magistrates they were each fined 10s.

Ashtead Woods, c. 1907. Rabbits also played a part in a very important discovery in Ashtead Woods in the 1920s. It was thought to be one that brought a Roman tile up from its burrow, leading to the discovery of a Roman house nineteen centuries old. The Ashtead villa was a corridor-type building with at least thirteen rooms, and a tile works that would have been dependent on the London market, transporting the tiles via Stane Street. Many of the tiles found had been laid out in the sun to harden and bore the footprints of dogs and cats.

Ashtead Woods were often visited by courting couples spending days out in the country. Local postcard makers obviously tried to encourage these visitors as this 1915 postcard shows!

Windy Corner, Ashtead Common, seen from the railway footbridge in 1939. The buildings of 1909 are still there (see page 69) but Woodfield House and surrounding area had been renamed 'Windy Corner'. This is with some justification as it faced a large open space to the north east. The site was still popular with day trippers who did not rely entirely on large caterers for their refreshments as many of the small cottages also served teas in their gardens and from their front windows. The track in front of the cottages led to Rushett Farm on the common and this was used to bring supplies to the bakery. The fan-shaped tree just visible on the horizon marks the highest point on the common and was known as 'The King Oak'.

Elm Cottage, The Common, *c.* 1950. This was built in the mid-nineteenth century as two three-roomed dwellings. The staircases went up into the single bedrooms above. About 1900 the building was converted into one cottage. It was condemned as unfit for human habitation in the 1930s, but it was not pulled down until 1968.

The Woodman, *c.* 1905. There has been a beerhouse in this position in Barnett Wood Lane, overlooking South Woodfield, since the middle of the nineteenth century, for the benefit of agricultural labourers and navvies who built and maintained the railway. By the end of the century the inn was the headquarters of the Ashtead quoits team, under the patronage of Charles Smithers, the publican (see page 106). As with so many public houses the interior and exterior have been altered a number of times. The publican seen standing in the doorway is Fred Samine.

Barnett Wood Lane, *c.* 1905. Appearing as far back as the seventeenth century, this road was known as Marsh Lane at the time. Although still relatively under-developed by the end of the nineteenth century, Ashtead Brickworks was established here in the 1880s and remained until about 1912. During the Second World War a surviving kiln was converted into a public air-raid shelter.

Grimditch and Webb Butchers, *c.* 1930. This shop was situated in Barnett Wood Lane and was one of three butchers in Ashtead at the time. They were in a long succession of butchers recorded in Ashtead, dating back to December 1695, when Sir Robert Howard's household accounts show that John Stone, butcher, was paid £1 13s 3d for a large delivery of beef and 2s 6d for killing a boar.

T. Steer, Barnett Wood Lane Stores, *c.* 1930. This shop, one of the few to remain unchanged in Ashtead for perhaps 100 years, stands on the corner of Glebe Road. As well as being a sub-post office from 1907 to 1950, no doubt the shop did a good trade in tobacco sales for men on their way to work and sweets for the children from the nearby council school.

Barnett Wood Lane, *c.* 1945. Around 1905 a developer called George Baker purchased the old brick field on the south side of Barnett Wood Lane and Church Road, seen here on the left, was laid out. George Baker also had a hall built in Church Road for use as a silent picture house, but the enterprise only survived a few years, the premises then being used as a skating rink.

Barnett Wood Lane, *c.* 1935. On the right of this photograph, the turning is Glebe Road, which was developed in 1887 on glebeland, forming part of New Purchase farmland. The twelve pairs of cottages were built for brickmakers and their families who worked in the brickworks, which was situated in the adjoining field.

Six
Churches and Schools

The Old Rectory, Rectory Lane, c. 1917.

St Giles' church, *c.* 1905. Situated on a former Roman site, the church began in about 1125 as a private chapel, built by a Norman lord, Lawrence of Rouen. Roman tiles can be seen in the south wall of the nave. In the early 1300s, Walter de Burleigh became Rector of Ashtead, living in the old parsonage, which stood on the corner of Skinners Lane and Ottways Lane, the garden stretching as far as where Maple Road stands today. The old parsonage was demolished around 1823.

St Giles' church, seen here in 1917, was rebuilt in the fifteenth and sixteenth centuries, and by 1523 the tower had been added. Between 1820 and 1877 Revd William Legge, Rector at the time, and Colonel and Mrs Mary Howard, Lord and Lady of the Manor, transformed the church inside and out. Amongst other alterations a porch and new entrance were built on the south side of the church.

St Giles' church, *c.* 1910. Although Ashtead was a relatively small village there could be large numbers of burials during times of sickness and epidemics. One of the saddest examples is that of Jethro Barnes, park keeper at Ashtead Park, and his wife Mary, who lost four of their six children within a few weeks in 1883 to scarlet fever. Ten years later, having had three more children, they had to endure the heartache of watching all three little girls die, again within a matter of weeks.

St Giles' church interior, *c.* 1905. During the Second World War the stained glass windows of St Giles' church suffered severe damage. The first bombs fell in Ashtead in August 1940, when the west window and the Denshire window in the chancel were damaged. In September further bombing destroyed the Howard window which was beside the pulpit. Sadly the Howard and Denshire windows were too badly damaged to be repaired, but the west window was taken away and repaired.

St Giles' church interior, *c.* 1907. During the same period of bombing, St Giles' School suffered land mine damage and classes were held in the church and vestry, as well as the Peace Memorial Hall and some private homes. Local residents remembered the sight of the blackboard set up in the aisle and the children dressed in their coats and mufflers, sitting in the pews. The school was repaired and reopened in 1941.

St Giles' church interior, c. 1932. Many of Ashtead's notable residents have been interred in family vaults in St Giles' church. The Howard family has a vault where several generations of the family are interred. The Smith and Denshire family vault is beneath the chancel. Among the members of the family buried here are two of Nathaniel and Hesther Smith's daughters, Anne and Elizabeth, who were both buried on 24 September 1838.

Revd William Legge, Rector of Ashtead from 1826 to 1872, was represented in this corbel over the west door, in recognition for the restoration work that was carried out on the church during his time as rector. A relative of Mary Howard, Revd Legge worked hard with her to try to improve conditions in the village.

The Hon. Mary Howard was also represented in a corbel over the west door, in gratitude for her generous donations towards the restoration of the church during her time as Lady of the Manor, from 1818 until her death at Ashtead Park in 1877.

Ashtead Burial Guild, 1895. Two years before this photograph was taken several parishioners, including John Fowler, who lived in Fowler's Cottage, Rectory Lane, formed a guild to provide a service for the departed of the parish. Earlier there had been a tendency for non-churchgoers to act as bearers at funerals and there had often been drunkenness afterwards. Members pictured outside the Old Rectory are, from left to right: G. Chitty, George Lisney, T. Goldsmith, J. May and John Fowler (secretary). One of the above smocks has been preserved and can be seen at Guildford museum.

Church Walk (seen here in 1930) is the ancient right of way to the medieval manor house which stood near the north-east corner of the church from the thirteenth century until about 1800. One of the manor house doors opened directly into the churchyard. After Sir Robert Howard built his new mansion around 1684, part of the old house was used as a dairy for many years. The cedar trees shown here are well over a hundred years old; sadly many were lost in the hurricane of 1987.

The Revd F.G.L. Lucas in 1904. Francis Lucas, the Rector of Ashtead parish from 1887 until 1906, was the son of Sir Thomas Lucas, Lord of the Manor from 1879 until 1889. He was a keen sportsman, playing for Ashtead Cricket Club with great success and held many local public offices, including District Councillor and president of Ashtead Working Men's Club. In 1902 Revd Lucas became a very wealthy man, being the sole benefactor in the will of Sir Thomas Lucas, inheriting an estate worth £775,984. In December 1906 the Revd R. Waddilove succeeded Revd Lucas as rector of Ashtead, who took up his duties in Suffolk. The parishioners presented him with a gold watch on his departure and, despite his enormous wealth, a cheque for £40!

St George's church, c. 1906. In 1882 a small iron church was given by Sir Thomas Lucas for the growing population in the north of the parish. In 1899 a fund was started for the building of a permanent church and by 1905 the iron church, standing on the corner of Oakfield Road, was moved on rollers to a site on the opposite side of the road and the building of a permanent church began. The new church was consecrated on 21 April 1906.

The Catholic church in 1965. In 1942 Ashtead's Catholics attended mass weekly in the Constitutional Hall in Barnett Wood Lane. Before this they had to travel to Epsom or Leatherhead. In 1944 the Roman Catholic Diocese of Southwark purchased a house called Mormead Shaw, which had suffered severe bomb damage, and services were held in its garage. By 1949 this ex-Army hut was erected for use as a church and the adjacent house, Rushmere, had been purchased as a presbytery.

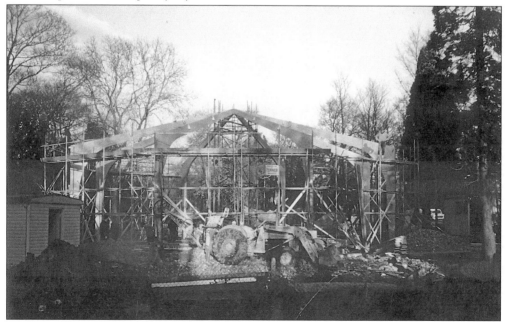

Building of the new church of St Michael the Archangel, 1966. In 1956 Fr Edward Maxwell was parish priest and plans were made for a permanent church, but sadly he died shortly before they materialized. Building commenced in 1966, and with Fr Bernard McGrath as parish priest, the new church opened in 1967, blessed by the Bishop of Arundel and Brighton on 27 October. Behind the church a new presbytery was added and in 1983 a parish hall was opened.

Children leaving St Giles' School, c. 1880. In 1852 the original part of the present school was built on land given by Mrs Mary Howard and erected at her expense. The school was then conveyed to the Rector of the parish and his successors for ever. Prior to this in Ashtead there had only been charity schools. One in Park Cottage in Park Lane was paid for by a bricklayer David White, who left money in his will for educational purposes, and donations from the Howard family. In 1818 it was attended by some seventy children under the care of James Penny and Elizabeth Huck.

St Giles' School, c. 1906. Initially the school was in three parts, infants, boys and girls, but the boys and girls were amalgamated in 1900, despite protests from the girls' mistress that although she would loyally do her part, she thought there was great moral harm in mixing the sexes. The head teacher recorded daily the problems of running the school, including the mystery of the missing dinners from the cloakroom, which was solved when a rat was found with its nose in one of the baskets!

St Giles' School pupils, *c.* 1906. The normal school day was 9 a.m. to midday and 2 p.m. to 4.30 p.m. with eight weeks' holiday a year. There were, however, often problems with attendance as children could be kept at home to help with work such as haymaking and in bad weather attendance often dropped due to problems with travelling to school. Until 1925 when a new school was built in Langley Bottom, sixty children from that area were driven to school in a horse-drawn wagon.

St Giles' School pupils, *c.* 1911. In 1900 gas replaced the old oil lamps but it was not until 1948 that electric lights were installed. In 1902 books and pencils replaced the slates previously used. Barnett Wood Lane School was opened in 1907, which relieved much of the pressure on St Giles' School, reducing the number of pupils to 166.

Parsons Mead, *c.* 1916. In 1859 Colonel Alexander Gleig purchased six acres of land between Leatherhead Road and Ottways Lane, and had Parsons Mead built on it. In 1861 Colonel Gleig, then a bachelor, lived in the house with two servants. In 1876 Frederick Peake, a London solicitor, rented the house, finally buying the property in 1880, from Colonel Gleig who had married by this time and was living in a new large house in Ottways Lane called The Hut.

Miss Jessie Elliston (1858-1942) from a painting on show in Parsons Mead School. In 1897 Jessie Elliston opened her first school in Woodfield Lane. Previously she had been governess at Leatherhead Vicarage. She bought Parsons Mead in Ottways Lane, paying for it by instalments, and it was to become one of the best-known schools in Ashtead. She must have been a very hardy lady because when war came in 1939, she was still helping to run the school, despite being well over eighty. Unfortunately she did not live to see peace again in this world as she died in 1942 at the age of eighty-four.

Pupils at Parsons Mead, 1906. The school opened in 1904 with forty-five girls aged between ten and eighteen; by the First World War there were ninety-five girls, both boarders and day pupils. During the First World War the girls and Miss Elliston put the grounds to good use keeping rabbits, pigs and fowls, as well as growing large amounts of fruit, picked by the pupils, to make up to 600lb of jam at a time.

Founder's Day at Parsons Mead School in 1947. The reputation of Parsons Mead continued to grow. Following Miss Elliston's death, radical changes occurred, including control of the school being handed over to a board of governors. The school's facilities have expanded greatly over the years, including the provision of an outdoor swimming pool in the 1960s and a new sports hall and science laboratory in the 1990s. Founder's Day is celebrated each year on a day close to Miss Elliston's birthday (31 May).

Ashtead boys' football team, 1923. The council school which opened in Barnett Wood Lane had a well-organized football team between the wars. All the above players have been identified and are, from left to right, back row: Mr Dyer, Arthur Haffington, Tom Newbury, Harold Winteridge, Alf Goodhew, Fred Etherington, Sir Arthur Glyn. Middle row: Albert Dorling, Frank Frewin, Percy Millman, Jack Fuller, Theo Hoyle. Front row: Reg Lifford, Ken Overington, Alf Cook.

Seven

Transport

Rebuilding the level crossing gates at Ashtead station in 1930.

The station, *c.* 1900. In 1847 the London, Brighton and South Coast Railway (LBSCR) extended the London and Croydon railway to the terminus at Upper High Street, Epsom. In 1856 the Epsom and Leatherhead Railway (E&LR) built a single line from this terminus to Leatherhead. A short time after this the Wimbledon and Dorking Railway took over this recently built line and in 1857 the London and South West Railway agreed to construct a double line along this route. Note the horse-drawn cab waiting at the station entrance.

A steam train at Ashtead station, *c.* 1900. The building of the line was started at the Leatherhead end and by February 1859 seven trains a day stopped at Ashtead station. In April 1859 Ashtead was given its first direct London service. Although the LSWR trains in their distinctive apple-green livery must have made a very impressive sight, some of Ashtead's residents opposed the railway. Mary Howard was said to have insisted the line was routed as far away as possible from Ashtead Park.

Station staff, *c.* 1900. The railways of Great Britain were run at the turn of the century by some half a million men on whose hard work and skill the entire system depended. It was, however, a dangerous job. In the last twenty-five years of the nineteenth century, 12,870 railway men were killed on duty, forty times greater than the number of railway passenger casualties. Accidents to railway workers were categorized as acts of God, as the companies were reluctant to accept responsibility for accidents among the staff. Despite all this, the service loyally drew families of men for generations. The stationmaster at Ashtead between 1873 and 1906 was Thomas Simms, assisted by his son William who worked as station clerk.

Railway station staff and fly drivers *c.* 1910. The fly drivers are distinguished by their top hats. They are, from left to right: Samuel Spence, Jim Cates, Charles Hogsden and Richard Perry. The boy seated is the ex-stationmaster's son, Oswald Simms. Why he chose to sit on the ground clutching a gun remains a mystery, although one possible explanation put forward is that part of his duties was shooting deer that had strayed onto the line.

Fly at Ashtead station, *c.* 1910. This type of quaint conveyance apparently did a good trade as there were several in operation at the time. The driver of this one was Charles Hogsden, a member of a well-known Ashtead family. Note the posters for Osenton's estate agents and the invitation to travel to the continent via Newhaven and Dieppe.

No. 314 *Charles C. Macrae* and the Portsmouth Express at Ashtead station, 19 August 1911. At this time on corridor trains the restaurant car would have been available for passengers. A good hot lunch could be purchased for 3s 6d and a typical menu in 1906 was soup, poached salmon, roast sirloin, roast chicken and salad all accompanied by the ceaseless tinkling of the knives and forks on the luncheon tables.

The stationmaster's house, *c.* 1910. This was the home of the Simms family for over twenty-five years. Julia Simms must have worked extremely hard looking after her large family in this small house. Her husband Thomas and son William would have to be turned out smartly in their uniforms, with white starched shirts, all in the days before constant hot water, when washing was done on a copper, clothes rubbed hard on a wooden scrubbing board and wrung out on a great iron mangle.

Ashtead Common from Station Bridge, c. 1910. The tea rooms on the common, such as Woodfield House, were ideally situated for excursionists arriving by train to spend the day in the countryside. Many children on days out from London would arrive on special excursion trains, which would then be shunted into the specially constructed sidings, shown here on the left of the photograph, until their return home at the end of the day.

Rebuilding the level crossing, 1930. On a Sunday morning, with trains passing slowly through, a large gang of railwaymen rebuilt the level crossing and gates which were now to be operated from the new signal box beside it. The whole operation was watched by a group of enthusiastic schoolboys. The scales on the platform came from a time when penny slot machines were very popular on stations, whether for purchasing chocolates, sweets, matches or even having your fortune told.

The new signal box, 1930. By 1925 electric trains passed through Ashtead from Waterloo, and this new signal box was followed by the construction of the new gates. Although in 1929 the steam train services from London Bridge had also been electrified, some goods trains and engineering steam trains still passed through Ashtead until the 1960s. The old semaphore signals at the level crossing were replaced by coloured lights in 1964.

The station, c. 1959. The goods yard on the right of this photograph was developed in 1903 but was to close a few years after this photograph was taken, in 1961, when the car park was constructed. One wonders how many train-spotting school boys would have stood at this point over the years, watching for the white plume of steam from the funnel as the train approached the station.

The station in 1959. The stationmaster's house had been given a smart coat of white paint by the time this photograph was taken, but by 1963 Ashtead's last stationmaster had vacated the house which was finally demolished in 1969. Many of the stationmasters who retired in the 1960s, as the jobs were being phased out, looked back with pleasure on the days when the railways were run with military precision and there was great pride in the industry.

The station, seen here in 1962, was built in 1885 and was typical of many of the attractive Victorian stations. They were often more elaborate than strictly necessary for the purpose, decorated with pretty gables and ornate cast iron pillars and fretwork. Considering that at this time the wealth of the country per head was very much less than today, it is amazing how well kept the stations were. Like so many other small stations at the time, Ashtead station was demolished in 1969 and the present building constructed.

Alfred Vanderbilt's stagecoach *The Venture* in The Street, 1914. Although motor buses and coaches were well established by this time, there were still stagecoaches on the streets. This one was run by an American millionaire. He died the following year, but a few coaches remained in service until the 1930s. A man in full livery would blow the post horn to herald the coach's approach and many residents still remember hearing it with pleasure during the quiet summer evenings. The Brewery Inn is on the right of the photograph.

George Astridge with delivery vans, *c.* 1905. In the early twentieth century the Astridge family of Ashtead developed a number of enterprises, one of which was haulage. This photograph shows George Astridge with one of his staff, Jim Cates, on the left. Later on, that side of the business was motorized and other family members branched out into the retail trade.

The landing of this early army aeroplane on Ashtead Common on 4 February 1914 obviously caused great excitement amongst Ashtead's residents. Understandably so, as this would have been a very unusual sight and probably the first time most people had seen an aeroplane at close proximity.

On 18 September 1914 ten double-decker London buses caused a stir in the area when they arrived at Epsom and Ashtead carrying 3,000 pieces of luggage. In preparation for the arrival of The University and Public Schools Brigade, their kit bags, Gladstone bags and dressing cases were placed on the pavement awaiting collection.

The Street, c. 1920. In 1914 a daily motor bus service was introduced between Clapham Common and Dorking, passing through Epsom and Ashtead. Until the 1930s many of the buses still had open tops and solid tyres like the one in this photograph. By 1924 the frequency of buses had increased greatly and it was now possible to travel directly to Morden, Guildford and West Croydon via Sutton.

The Street, c. 1928. In what appears to be a rush-hour scene, a new single-decker bus is travelling through The Street, but old open-topped buses are still in service. In 1927 the 418 route was introduced between Epsom and Effingham, running half-hourly along Woodfield Lane, extending to West Ewell and then Tolworth by 1930. This was the first bus serving The Pond and Lower Ashtead area.

The Street, 1950s. After the time this photograph was taken, car ownership increased greatly and this led to the gradual decline in bus services in the area. The main services which run through Ashtead today, routes 408 and 479, which replaced route 418, have decreased in frequency each year.

Leatherhead Road, c. 1938. With the increase in car ownership, the traffic had increased greatly on the main A24. In the 1930s there were plans to build an Ashtead bypass, running from the Epsom Road, through a corner of Ashtead Park, along Dene Road to rejoin the A24 at The Warren, on the left of this photograph. The houses built in Dene Road at the corner of Grove Road were set well back from the road in preparation for the road, but plans to build the bypass were abandoned in 1977.

Eight
Sport and Leisure

A coursing meet in the fields adjacent to Park Lane, *c.* 1910.

Rose Garden Bathing Pool (also known as the Floral Swimming Pool) in the late 1920s. In the early twentieth century there was a large clay pit at the railway end of Green Lane, off Barnett Wood Lane. The area also contained a large house and kilns for the manufacture of bricks. The excavation became very deep and eventually a spring was struck and the pit filled with water. This put an end to the brickworks, but the owner, Mr Henry Weller, turned one acre of water into a swimming pool with steps, a raft and a diving board.

Henry Weller also provided refreshment facilities and a tennis court. The pool was so popular that people came down from London, usually by train, and on fine weekends the attendance sometimes reached 3,000. The pool was 30ft deep at one point and although there were no fatalities through drowning, Frederick Hampton, a young scout, saved two boys from drowning, and was presented with a bronze medal of the Royal Humane Society by Mrs Pantia Ralli at Ashtead Park.

The Floral Pool closed in 1959 after more than forty years of use and the site, together with a nearby nursery, was sold for development.

Quoits players, *c.* 1885. The game was played with iron rings which had to be thrown a distance of 18 yards to encircle, if possible, a pin or a 'hob' protruding from a patch of damp clay, to win two points. If this was not achieved the player, or side, whose quoit was the nearest to the hob gained one point. The Ashtead team was based at the Woodman, under the patronage of Charles Smithers, the landlord, seated in the centre of the group.

A coursing meet, *c*. 1910. Coursing for hares was a popular sport in days gone by. Dating back to 1500 BC it is occasionally indulged in today, despite attempts to have it banned. The game, usually a hare, is pursued by hounds, often greyhounds, that hunt by sight rather than scent. Greyhound racing has developed from coursing. The coursing season ran from September to March and took place in the fields off Park Lane. Despite its rough associations, coursing for hares seemed to require a certain sartorial elegance – Sunday best suits, gold watch chains and occasionally bowler hats instead of cloth caps. From left to right: Bruce Sayer, Ralph Steere, Ralph Sayer, -?-. Bruce and Ralph Sayer are the grandsons of George and Maria Sayer from the Brewery Inn (see p. 13).

Below opposite: Ashtead cricket team, 1908. The only identified player is Fred Bailey, who is in a semi-recumbent position, holding the ball. Possibly the club was celebrating its twenty-first birthday on this bank holiday fixture, since it was founded in March 1887. Many famous players have appeared on the club's ground in Woodfield Lane. They include Jack Hobbs, Walter Hammond and Denis Compton. The ground has also been used for tennis, football and celebratory events.

Ashtead Football Club, 1914. A team of young Ashtead men are celebrating what must have been a successful season. It is sad to think that their plans for the following one were to be curtailed and some of these faces would not be seen again six years later. The captain was John Brooker, on his right is Frank Steere and behind the latter is H. Wyatt.

Ashtead Football Club, 1922. By this time football was again a well-supported recreation after the war years. The side must have been a strong one in the 1921/22 season as it recorded a triumph by winning the Sutton and District Charity Cup. Later the club left the Craddocks Lane ground and settled at the recreation ground in Barnett Wood Lane.

Football teams of the University and Public Schools Brigade, based at Ashtead and Leatherhead, 1915. Brigadier-General Gordon Gilmour, commanding officer of the brigade, organized a challenge cup to be competed for by various companies. On Saturday 6 February 1915, B Company 20th Battalion, based at Leatherhead, defeated C Company 21st Battalion, based at Ashtead, by 5 goals to 3 in the final played at Epsom Recreation Ground.

The Donkey Derby, c. 1912. The Ashtead Cricket Ground in Woodfield Lane was the setting for events other than cricket. In the summer it also saw locally organized fêtes whose attractions would include races and fancy dress competitions. From the photograph it would appear that the two events were sometimes combined. Fred Bailey, an enthusiastic local sportsman, is seen winning the donkey derby, apparently by about two lengths. It is not known how he got on in the fancy dress competition.

Two Ashtead Girl Guides, 1919. Myrtle and Ivy Chapman, pictured here, were members of the 1st Ashtead Girl Guide Company, which was formed in the previous year. The company met in the old iron church of St George's, which they shared with the Scouts. A Brownie pack was started in 1923. Since 1933 the meetings have taken place at the Guide Headquarters behind the Constitutional Hall.

Ashtead Life Boys, late 1940s. The Life Boys were the junior branch of the Boys' Brigade and their leader from 1940 until 1976 was Miss Lilian Stainer of Craddocks Avenue, seen here with her assistant, Miss Deacon. The boys had a uniform with a nautical touch, with sailor caps and lanyards. The Brigade continued until 1987, when staffing shortages caused it to close.

Nine
The War Years

The 21st Battalion Royal Fusiliers at Woodfield House, 1914.

UNIVERSITY & PUBLIC SCHOOLS BRIGADE

5000 MEN AT ONCE

The Old Public School and University Men's Committee makes an urgent appeal to their fellow Public School and University men

to at once enlist in these battalions, thus upholding the glorious traditions of their Public Schools & Universities.

TERMS OF SERVICE.

Age on enlistment 19 to 35, ex-soldiers up to 45, and certain ex-non-commissioned officers up to 50. Height 5 ft. 3 in. and upwards. Chest 34 in. at least. Must be medically fit.

General Service for the War.

Men enlisting for the duration of the War will be discharged with all convenient speed at the conclusion of the War

PAY AT ARMY RATES.

and all married men or widowers with children will be accepted, and will draw separation allowance under Army Conditions.

HOW TO JOIN.

Men wishing to join should apply at once, personally, to the Public Schools & Universities Force, 66, Victoria Street, Westminster, London, S.W., or the nearest Recruiting Office of this Force.

GOD SAVE THE KING !

The declaration of war on 4 August 1914 was the occasion for the first appeal for 100,000 men to join the colours. Men from many towns, professions and occupations with similar interests volunteered to join special battalions. During August men with a public school and university background agreed they too would form such a battalion, and by 12 September the 5,000 hoped-for strength was easily achieved. The War Office decided to enlist the men in four battalions.

The 21st Battalion marching in Ashtead Park. On 18 September 1914 the 18th, 19th and half of the 20th Battalions, The Royal Fusiliers (University and Public Schools Brigade) arrived in Epsom, where they were to be billeted. The remaining half of the 20th Battalion were billeted at Leatherhead and on 24 September, 2,000 men of the 21st Battalion arrived in Ashtead, under the command of Lieutenant-Colonel J. Stuart-Wortley.

The 21st Battalion on parade on Ashtead Common. Private William Horne wrote to *The Whitby Gazette*, where he had worked as a journalist before the war, describing the routine: 'We commence at 7 a.m. and have drill, breakfast at 8 a.m. and resume drill at 9.30 a.m. Dinner at 12.15 followed by a light rest until 2.30 p.m., when the whole battalion falls in on the parade ground – Ashtead Common – for a route march which lasts until 5 p.m., when we are free until next morning.'

(C.Coy) 4th Batt. P.S. Royal Fusiliers, marching to Church Parade.

Johnson's Ashtead, P.O. Series. 10.

The 21st Battalion on route march in Woodfield Lane. Private Horne continues in his letter to *The Whitby Gazette*: 'The real enjoyment is the route march. 1,200 men marching in companies, four abreast. It is glorious marching along these lanes of Surrey, with their lofty trees and high overhanging hedges, off which we manage to gather blackberries as we pass.'

3348. No. 3. Company, P.S. Batt. R.F. Marching, Ashtead.

Johnson's Ashtead. P.O. Series.

The 21st Battalion marching past the Brewery Inn. Further down The Street the Union Jack is flying outside Harry Johnson's post office. Harry Johnson, who produced nearly all the postcards of the University and Public Schools Brigade, would develop the photographs and have them on sale in his shop within 24 hours.

The 21st Battalion on parade opposite St Giles' School, 1914. The men of the UPS found they had fallen into extremely comfortable billeting arrangements. All Ashtead's residents gave them a cordial welcome. Four of the men were billeted at Parsons Mead, the coach house being turned into quarters for them during term time, and during the holidays they moved into the house. Men were also billeted at St Giles' School, pictured here.

Officers of the 21st Battalion at Forest Lodge. Officers were billeted in the comfort of Forest Lodge, which was also used as their headquarters. Pictured here is the owner, Augustus Meyers, who purchased the estate in 1901 and lived there for fifty years. He had the present Forest Lodge built further back from the road than the original house which was a conversion of the old Haunch of Venison inn. Although this old house was demolished at that time, the rise in the main Epsom Road is still known as Haunch Hill.

Men of the 21st Battalion on the lake in Ashtead Park. As well as drill and route marches, lectures were given to the officers and men at Ashtead on military subjects such as 'Hints Regarding Life In Camp'. They also received talks on general subjects, among others 'The Health Of The Soldier' and 'The Kaiser As I Knew Him'! After 5 p.m., when the men were free for the rest of the day, they were able to enjoy leisure pursuits, including boating, pictured here, and walks on Ashtead Common or to Box Hill.

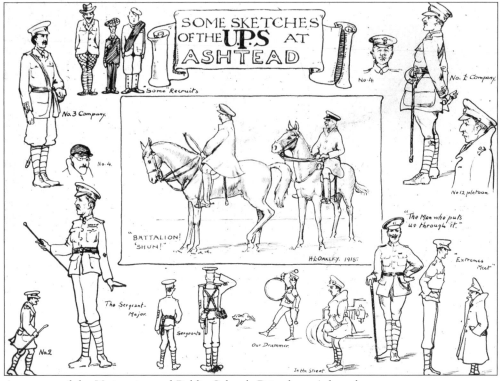

A cartoon of the University and Public Schools Brigade at Ashtead.

King George V in Ashtead Park. On 11 October the first rifles were received, 200 to each battalion, and on 13 October, King George V inspected the brigade. The 18th and 19th Battalions paraded on Epsom Downs, after which the King went to Ashtead Park to inspect the 21st Battalion and on to Leatherhead where the 20th Battalion paraded.

The 21st Battalion in Ashtead Park. The University and Public Schools Brigade was one of the most democratic in the Army. Nearly all the men started level and were promoted according to ability. By November 1914, when work had started on Woodcote Park Camp, several hundred men had left the brigade to take up commissions and 170 more recruits had been posted to the 21st Battalion. By Christmas 1914 the men had now been in their billets for fifteen weeks and many had made close friendships with their hosts.

On 25 November 1914, work began on the building of the camp adjoining Headley Road and Chalk Pit Road, now The Ridgeway. Twenty-four huts were built for each battalion, 120ft long by 20ft wide, each accommodating fifty men. Private Reg Dalton wrote to his parents in Birmingham: 'I was working on the roof of the hut on the right and saw this photo being taken, so I rushed into it.' Reg is standing in the front row on the left with the pipe.

Woodcote Park Camp. The road running between the huts from the Headley Road entrance was called by the men 'The Street', showing the affection they held for Ashtead, their adopted village. Many other buildings were erected, including the dining room, reading room, cook houses, doctors' consulting rooms and bath and shower houses. A power station at one corner provided the electricity supply. By April 1915 the entire brigade had moved into the completed camp.

The 21st Battalion at Woodcote Park Camp. On Tuesday 11 May 1915 the four battalions of the UPS departed from Epsom Downs station for camp at Clipstone. Woodcote Park Camp was to become a convalescent hospital for Canadian troops until the end of the war. The men of the UPS missed the beautiful countryside of Surrey and all the friends they had made. Lieutenant Colin Hurry wrote this poem, which appeared in the Brigade magazine, remembering their days here:

To Epsom, Ashtead and Leatherhead

Come, sing with me
To the peerless three,
Goddesses blithe and gay.
Come, sing with me
To the Trinity
Hallowed and far away.
Come, sing with me
Though far we be
Up in the chilly North.
Some day will see
Us fair and free
Sallying gaily forth.
Perchance in mufti – who knows and when? –
Back from the ranks, acquitted men,
Back to the sunny South again,
Back to the peerless three.

Reunion of the 21st Battalion at Ashtead in 1931. Following their time at Clipstone the 21st Battalion left for France on 14 November 1915. They had several spells in the trenches at Béthune, and although there were no major actions at the time, eighteen men were killed either by snipers' bullets or stray shells. On 25 February 1916 the battalion was disbanded and the men transferred to other battalions or regiments. Reg Dalton, after serving as a Corporal in the Royal Engineers, survived to return to his family in Birmingham. William Horne, after serving in France with the 12th Battalion Royal Fusiliers, escaped injury and returned to his job as a journalist with *The Whitby Gazette*. Although as an officer in the Army Service Corps Colin Hurry spent the Armistice in a field hospital in Basra in modern Iraq, suffering from fever and jaundice, he eventually recovered to return home to his new wife in Birkenhead. All three men were able to join the Old 21st Association, and fulfil their wartime wish of returning to Ashtead, in March 1931, to present Revd E. Austin, Rector of St Giles' church, with the photograph below in gratitude for the residents' hospitality.

Peace celebrations, 1919. Although the fighting in the First World War ended with the Armistice of 11 November 1918, the conflict was not officially over until the Treaty of Versailles on 28 June 1919 and many places in the country held festivals of remembrance soon after. Ashtead chose to celebrate on August Bank Holiday, which was on 4 August that year, a significant date as it was five years to the day after the declaration of war.

The day opened with a peal of church bells and at midday lunch was served to 250 ex-servicemen at Barnett Wood Lane School. A fancy dress competition was organized and contestants gathered on Woodfield to march to the cricket ground in Woodfield Lane where the judging took place. The first prize, a sugar basin, went to a girl called Lila Denman, who was in a costume representing 'Peace'.

Floral tributes were laid at the temporary cenotaph nearby and sports and entertainments for children and adults followed. The children were served tea in a marquee and each received a souvenir. There was dancing on the green to music provided by a military band and the day ended with a firework display.

The sixty-two Ashtead men who gave their lives during the First World War were remembered at this ceremony to open the Peace Memorial Hall in 1924. A particularly sad story is that of Frank Hicks, son of Alan Hicks, captain of Ashtead fire brigade. Frank was a young man who was born and lived all his life in Ashtead. Shortly after his eighteenth birthday in 1914, he was serving as a lieutenant in the 4th Battalion Royal Fusiliers and in May 1915 sustained shrapnel wounds at Ypres. Suffering from all the distressing symptoms of severe shell shock, it took Frank nearly two years of hospital treatment and rest at his home in Great Murrays, Agates Lane, to recover. This incredibly brave young man returned to France in 1917 and went on to be awarded the Military Cross for gallantry before being tragically killed in action on 21 August 1918, at just twenty-one years old.

Captain Henry Reynolds VC, MC, of the 12th Battalion the Royal Scots Regiment. After the outbreak of the First World War, Henry Reynolds enlisted in the Royal Scots Regiment on 5 October 1914. On 12 April 1917 he was awarded the Military Cross for a series of actions. On 20 September 1917 , at Passchendaele, his company suffered heavy casualties from an enemy 'pill box'. Captain Reynolds proceeded alone crawling from shell hole to shell hole, all the time being under heavy machine-gun fire, until at the pill box entrance he forced a grenade inside. Afterwards although wounded he organized his men and led them to a further objective, capturing seventy prisoners and two machine guns. For these actions Captain Reynolds was awarded the Victoria Cross by the King at Buckingham Palace.

Henry Reynolds was born on 16 August 1881 and married in 1905 having three children. Following his retirement from the Army in 1927, Henry's life was touched with tragedy. His only son, Thomas, a lieutenant in the Royal Scots Regiment, was killed in a traffic accident in India in 1931, and his eldest daughter, Gwendolen, after marrying a lieutenant in the Royal Tank Regiment, died in India in 1935. Despite his personal tragedies Henry spent the rest of his life helping ex-servicemen, working as superintendent of Sir Frederick Milner Homes in Beckenham, then in Ermyn Way in Leatherhead. The present Milner House home for the elderly is situated there today. Henry Reynolds died on 26 March 1948 and is buried here in St Giles' churchyard.

Ashtead Royal British Legion, 1924. Formed in this year, the Ashtead branch of the Royal British Legion has helped ex-servicemen and women over the years as well as organizing many social activities. They have also been responsible for maintaining the war memorial and refurbishing it in 1990/91. The members in this photograph are seated in the back garden of Ashtead Lodge, Parkers Hill, home of Brigadier-General E. Gascoigne.

The Ashtead Special Constabulary photographed in the garden of The Old Bakery (which was the section leader Fred Goldsmith's home) in 1939. From left to right: Fred Goldsmith, George Cook, Harry Barrows, Harry Chitty, Davidson, Bert Goldsmith, E. Gritt, H. Edwards, H. Pateman, W. Ayliffe, Jack Worsfold.

Bomb damage in Gaywood Road, 1940. On 26 August 1940 the first bombs fell in Ashtead. Although no one was killed or injured, damage was caused to thirty-five houses. A few days later on 30 August, sixty high-explosive bombs were dropped in a line from Leatherhead to Ashtead, in a daylight raid, killing five people and causing many injuries. These houses in Gaywood Road sustained the worst damage. Pictured here is one of the residents, Bert Oliver.

Among the houses destroyed was this house in Gaywood Road, home of the Bailey family. On the same day, St Giles' School, the windows of St Giles' church and surrounding houses suffered serious damage. Although not suffering to the same extent as towns nearer London, more bombs continued to be dropped in Ashtead, including one in March 1941, when St Andrew's School was destroyed by a landmine. Following a quieter few years, there were more attacks from the new doodlebugs and the last bomb to drop on Ashtead was a V-2 rocket which caused one minor casualty and damage to houses in Park Lane.

Bomb damage in Purcells Close, 1940. All Ashtead's residents joined in the enthusiastic support for the war effort. To combat food rationing people grew their own vegetables and war allotments were set up on land off Craddocks Avenue. In October 1941 a British Restaurant was started in the recreation ground off Barnett Wood Lane, providing a sustaining meal very cheaply. Children from Streatham and Dulwich were evacuated to Ashtead and the residents with their usual hospitality welcomed these children in their homes.

Ashtead Home Guard, seen here in June 1943, was formed in response to Sir Anthony Eden's appeal at a time when a German invasion seemed a very real threat. The sixty volunteers in Ashtead's company were under Major Aitken and based in The Marld. One of their duties was to ensure that blackout regulations were followed and that the dark curtains at windows were in place. In this photograph, from left to right, are: Ron Main, Arthur Kemp and John Thorpe with a sprocket mortar.

Civil Defence Workers in 1945. In the late 1930s, with the threat of an outbreak of war, local authorities were ordered to organize squads of air-raid wardens, rescue workers and first-aid staff for any emergency which might arise. In many parts of the country civil defence was hardly needed as there were no air raids but that was not true for Ashtead. This photograph shows some of the people of the Civil Defence and ARP outside St Giles' School, Dene Road.

VE Day Party, Culverhay, May 1945. Scenes of celebration like this were repeated all over Ashtead at the end of the Second World War. On 8 May 1945 Ashtead's residents also remembered the seventy men from the village who had been killed on active service, with a special service at St Giles' church. In the Ashtead and Leatherhead area during the Second World War, 611 bombs were dropped causing severe damage to 282 houses and the destruction of 71. They had caused injury to 138 civilians, of whom 61 were seriously injured, and 11 people had been killed.

Acknowledgements

Grateful thanks are due to the following people who allowed the use of photographs and supplied information:

The Leatherhead and District Local History Society, especially Mr Jack Willis whose own research into the identities of so many individuals and places was invaluable to many of the captions.

Miss Paula Chitty, Mrs Joan Cooper, Lady Hayter, Mrs Catherine Larthe, Lens of Sutton, Major R.P. Mason, The Royal Scots Regimental Headquarters, Mrs Monica McAllistair, Mrs Jean Ralli, Mr Meredith Worsfold.

All the residents of Ashtead, past and present, who have so generously donated photographs to the Leatherhead and District Local History Society.

Bibliography

Bygone Ashtead, Geoffrey Gollin.
A History of Firefighting, Evan Green Hughes.
Ashtead, A Village Transformed, Alan A. Jackson.
Kelly's Directories of Surrey.
The Royal Fusiliers In The Great War, H.C. O'Neill.
A History of Paddocks Way from The Ashtead Resident, Nicholas Rule.
The History of Ashtead Park, F.E. Pezzey & H.G. Murrell.
A History of Ashtead, J.C. Stuttard.
The History of The Royal Fusiliers UPS, *The Times*.
Travelling By Train In The Edwardian Age, Phillip Unwin.
Ashtead. The Street in the 1920s, Meredith Worsfold.
The Sutton Journal and District Advertiser.
The Sutton, Cheam and Epsom Advertiser.
The Surrey Magazine.